WG

The Book of
New York Wisdom

The Book of
New York Wisdom

Common Sense and Uncommon Genius
From 101 Great New Yorkers

Compiled and Edited by Criswell Freeman

WALNUT GROVE PRESS
Nashville, TN
(615) 256-8584

ISBN 1-887655-16-6

Printed in the United States of America
Cover Design by Mary Mazer
Typesetting & Page Layout by Sue Gerdes
Edited by Alan Ross and Angela Beasley
1 2 3 4 5 6 7 8 9 10 • 96 97 98 99

ACKNOWLEDGMENTS
The author gratefully acknowledges the helpful support of Angela Beasley, Dick and Mary Freeman, and Mary Susan Freeman.

For Glenda and Bill Norvell

Table of Contents

Introduction

As a boy, I began collecting quotations on 3x5 cards. It was not until years later that I realized fully half of my collection came from New Yorkers. Why? Because New Yorkers are so quotable and so often quoted.

This book features the humor and insights of 101 great New Yorkers. Additionally, I've spared room for a few near-greats and a small gaggle of sightseers (who, like me, are fascinated by the Empire State).

The quoted sources in this book represent a cross section of the entire state; not surprisingly, the renowned and ancient city of Gotham is well represented.

New Yorkers, when taken together, compose possibly the most quotable collection of human beings in the history of mankind. So if you're looking for a helpful saying or a well-turned phrase, look no further than New York. If you can't find it there, you can't find it anywhere.

1

All-Purpose Advice

Plato wrote, "Advice is a sacred thing." If so, New York must be a very sacred place because advice, it seems, is everywhere. From the Big Apple to the Adirondacks, the Empire State is a awash in wise counsel.

What follows is all-purpose advice from in-the-know New Yorkers. If you take these words to heart, you will enrich your life. If you ignore this chapter and suffer the consequences, don't blame Plato.

The supply of advice
always exceeds the demand.

Josh Billings

Advice is what we ask for
when we already know the answer
but wish we didn't.

Erica Jong

Advice is like castor oil — easy to give
but dreadful to take.

Josh Billings

Study the game, accept advice, keep fit,
and above all, save your money.

Babe Ruth

Think health — eat sparingly,
exercise regularly, walk a lot,
and think positively about yourself.

Norman Vincent Peale

Keep your weight down,
and keep your hair cut.

Jackie Onassis

Think and you won't sink.

B. C. Forbes

Become a possibilitarian.
See possibilities — always see them
for they're always there.

Norman Vincent Peale

Get to know yourself,
your failings, passions, and prejudices, so you
can separate them from what you see.

Bernard Baruch

Look past the glitter,
beyond the showmanship, to the reality,
the hard substance of things.

Mario Cuomo

Have a scrupulous anxiety to do right.

Joseph Pulitzer

Train up a child
in the way he should go —
and walk there yourself
once in a while.

Josh Billings

You can't change the past.
Too many folks spend their lives trying to fix
things that happened before their time.
You're better off using your time
to improve yourself.

Sadie Delany

Cultivate only the habits
that you are willing should master you.

Elbert Hubbard

Teach the nobility of labor and the beauty
of human service.

Peter Cooper

Have a sincere desire to serve God
and mankind, then start living by faith.

Norman Vincent Peale

Truth is the only safe ground to stand upon.
Elizabeth Cady Stanton

Trust yourself, be what you are,
and do what you ought to do the way you
should do it. You have got to discover you,
what you do, and trust it.
Barbara Streisand

At least ten times every day affirm,
"I expect the best and, with God's help,
I will attain the best."
Norman Vincent Peale

Keep your eyes on the stars
and your feet on the ground.
Theodore Roosevelt

As long as you're going to be thinking
anyway, think big.
Donald Trump

Follow the path of the unsafe,
　　　independent thinker.

Thomas J. Watson

You might as well fall flat on your face
　　　as lean over too far backward.

James Thurber

Throw your heart over the fence,
　　　and the rest will follow.

Norman Vincent Peale

Live truth instead of professing it.

Elbert Hubbard

 Be simple.

> *Alfred E. Smith*

 Cut back on your possessions.
> The more you own, the more time
> you waste taking care of things.
>> *Bessie & Sadie Delany*

 Nobody ever lost money taking a profit.
> *Bernard Baruch*

 Buying on credit is like drinking too much.
> The buzz happens immediately.
> The hangover comes the day after.
>> *Dr. Joyce Brothers*

 Don't spend what you don't have.
Forget credit cards — they are the devil's work.
> *Bessie & Sadie Delany*

What we should do is not "future" ourselves
to death. We should "now" ourselves more.
"Now thyself," is more important than
"Know thyself."

Mel Brooks

Resist growing up!

B. C. Forbes

No matter how long you live, die young.

Elbert Hubbard

Don't simply retire from something.
Have something to retire to.

Harry Emerson Fosdick

Never tell them
what you wouldn't do.

Adam Clayton Powell

Fill what's empty. Empty what's full.
Scratch where it itches.

Alice Roosevelt Longworth

Vote for the man who promises the least.

Bernard Baruch

Most successful people are early risers.
To get up in the world,
get up early in the morning.

B. C. Forbes

Go to bed.
What you're staying up
for isn't worth it.

Andy Rooney

2

Happiness

In her day, no American poet was more beloved than Ella Wheeler Wilcox. Wilcox and her husband spent winters entertaining artists and writers in New York. The rest of the year, Ella dispensed down-home advice through inspirational verse. Eight decades after death, her poems continue to uplift.

Wilcox had a straightforward approach to happiness. She wrote,

Laugh and the world laughs with you;
Weep and you weep alone;
For the sad old earth must borrow its mirth;
But has trouble enough of its own.

The following quotations enlighten us on that most important of topics: happiness. Take these lessons to heart, and you'll never be alone for long.

When you're not thinking about yourself,
you're usually happy.

Al Pacino

Happiness is a habit. Cultivate it.

Elbert Hubbard

Don't mistake pleasure for happiness.

Josh Billings

Happiness doesn't depend
upon who you are or what you have;
it depends upon what you think.

Dale Carnegie

An inexhaustible good nature is
one of the most precious gifts of heaven.

Washington Irving

If you make friends with yourself,
you will never be alone.

Maxwell Maltz

Talk happiness. The world is sad enough
without your woe.

Ella Wheeler Wilcox

Pessimism is a waste of time.

Norman Cousins

Happiness is not a goal.
It is a by-product.

Eleanor Roosevelt

Jealousy is a mental cancer.

B. C. Forbes

Cynicism is intellectual treason.

Norman Cousins

Be paranoid in reverse.
Suspect people of plotting
to make you happy.

J. D. Salinger

Each of us makes his own weather.

Bishop Fulton J. Sheen

One face to the world, another at home makes for misery.

Amy Vanderbilt

Misery is a communicable disease.

Martha Graham

Nobody can make you feel inferior without your consent.

Eleanor Roosevelt

What you have outside you counts less than what you have inside you.

B. C. Forbes

Too many people overvalue what they're not and undervalue what they are.

Malcolm Forbes

When what we are is what we want to be,
that is happiness.

Malcolm Forbes

The most effective way to ensure the value
of the future is to confront the present
courageously and constructively.

Rollo May

Success is getting what you want.
Happiness is wanting what you get.

Dale Carnegie

It is easy to get everything you want,
provided you first learn to do without
the things you cannot get.

Elbert Hubbard

I never want to get used to something
I may someday have to do without.

Fred Allen

For me, a healthy belly laugh is one
of the most beautiful sounds in the world.

Bennett Cerf

Please, Lord, teach us to laugh again;
but God, never let us forget that we cried.

Bill Wilson

Never lose your sense of humor.
The happiest people are the ones
who are able to laugh at themselves.

Bessie & Sadie Delany

Good temper,
like a sunny day,
sheds light
on everything.

Washington Irving

Painting's not important.
The important thing is keeping busy.

Grandma Moses

A man who works with his hands is a laborer.
A man who works with his hands and his head
is a craftsman. A man who works with his hands
and his head and his heart is an artist.

Louis Nizer

Happiness lies in the joy of achievement
and the thrill of creative effort.

Franklin D. Roosevelt

Follow your bliss.

Joseph Campbell

A man is as good as what he loves.

Saul Bellow

Peace is always beautiful.

Walt Whitman

The place to be happy is here.
The time to be happy is now.
The way to be happy
is to make others happy.

Robert Ingersoll

Don't put off until tomorrow
what can be enjoyed today.

Josh Billings

The trick is growing up
without growing old.

Casey Stengel

The ability to be in the present
is a major component of mental wellness.

Abraham Maslow

Live in day-tight compartments.

Dale Carnegie

3

Courage

The most storied contest between two New Yorkers didn't take place in Madison Square Garden. In fact, it didn't take place in New York at all. The Empire State's most historic fight, the duel between Aaron Burr and Alexander Hamilton, occurred across the river on a dueling field at Weehawken, New Jersey.

In 1804, Burr challenged Hamilton, and the two men faced off at ten paces. Burr shot, Hamilton died, and Burr became a social outcast. So much for the wisdom of dueling.

While his insights on proper resolution of personal discord may be called into question, no one can dispute Hamilton's brilliance on matters political. Two centuries after his death, his writings remain classic commentaries on American constitutional law.

Hamilton once observed, "Those who stand for nothing will fall for anything." In the quotations that follow, notable New Yorkers teach us about the futility of fear. Their advice is important because the recipe for happiness includes a heaping helping of courage.

The first and greatest commandment is:
Don't let them scare you!

Elmer Davis

The greatest mistake you can make is
to be continually fearing
you will make one.

Elbert Hubbard

We have nothing to fear but fear itself.

Franklin D. Roosevelt

You must do the thing
you think you cannot do.

Eleanor Roosevelt

Never let the fear
of striking out
get in your way.

Babe Ruth

Courage is the ladder
    on which all other virtues mount.

Clare Boothe Luce

You may be disappointed if you fail,
    but you are doomed if you don't try.

Beverly Sills

You gain strength, courage and confidence
    every time you look fear in the face.

Eleanor Roosevelt

To escape criticism,
    do nothing, say nothing, be nothing.

Elbert Hubbard

Death is not the enemy.
Living in constant fear of it is.

Norman Cousins

Fear is the absence of faith.

Paul Tillich

As many people die from
an excess of timidity as from
an excess of bravery.

Norman Mailer

The worst of all fears is the fear of living.

Theodore Roosevelt

Only those who dare to fail greatly
can ever achieve greatly.

Robert F. Kennedy

In modern society, the opposite of courage
is not cowardice. It is conformity.

Rollo May

Decision is a risk
rooted in the courage of being free.

Paul Tillich

Worry is a state of mind based on fear.

Napolean Hill

If you want to conquer fear,
don't sit at home and think about it.
Go out and get busy.

Dale Carnegie

The thing we fear
we bring to pass.

Elbert Hubbard

Have the daring to accept yourself as
a bundle of possibilities, and undertake the
game of making the most of your best.

Harry Emerson Fosdick

Do not look for approval except for
the consciousness of doing your best.

Bernard Baruch

Teach yourself to work in uncertainty.

Bernard Malamud

Never turn back
until the thing is accomplished.

Ulysses S. Grant

Start with what is right
rather than what is acceptable.

Peter Drucker

In the truest sense, freedom cannot
be bestowed, it must be achieved.

Franklin D. Roosevelt

Far better it is to dare mighty things, to win
glorious triumphs even though checkered by
failures, than to rank with those poor spirits
who neither enjoy much nor suffer much
because they live in the gray twilight that
knows no victory or defeat.

Theodore Roosevelt

The only limit to our realization of tomorrow
will be our doubts of today.

Franklin D. Roosevelt

Telling a lie is a sign of fear.
It means you can't face up to something.
If you tell a lie, ask yourself
what you are afraid of.

Bessie Delany

Confidence is contagious.

Vince Lombardi

In crisis the most daring course
is often the safest.

Henry Kissinger

When you get to the end of your rope,
tie a knot and hang on.

Franklin D. Roosevelt

4

Others

Largely ignored by his contemporaries, Herman Melville spent the last twenty years of his professional life as a New York customs inspector. By the time of Melville's death, even his metaphorical epic *Moby Dick* was all but forgotten.

Contemporaneously, an upstate auctioneer named Henry Wheeler Shaw adopted the pen name Josh Billings and began writing humorous essays. The light-hearted Billings became an instant celebrity, proving once and for all that you can't judge a book by its coverage.

Despite their different approaches to the written word, Josh Billings and Herman Melville did agree on the importance of community. Melville, true to his style, wrote, "We cannot live only for ourselves. A thousand fibers connect us with our fellow men." Billings simply observed, "Solitude is a good place to visit but a poor place to stay."

In this chapter, knowledgeable New Yorkers discuss the ethical treatment of other people. Whether you're in the mood for maximum metaphors or metaphorical maxims, read on.

Life is an exercise in forgiveness.

Norman Cousins

Forgiveness is the final form of love.

Reinhold Niebuhr

Forgiving presupposes remembering.

Paul Tillich

Hating people is like burning down
your own house to get rid of a rat.

Harry Emerson Fosdick

Bitterness imprisons life;
love releases it.

Harry Emerson Fosdick

A retentive memory is a good thing,
but the ability to forget is
the true token of greatness.

Elbert Hubbard

The main regrets I have found in my 100 years
of living come when I haven't treated
someone as well as I could have.

Bessie Delany

One of the most time consuming things
is to have an enemy.

E. B. White

Love looks through a telescope,
envy through a microscope.

Josh Billings

Jealousy is the tribute mediocrity
pays to genius.

Bishop Fulton J. Sheen

It's easy to manage our neighbor's
business — it's your own that's tough.

Josh Billings

Every man should have a fair-sized cemetery
in which to bury the faults of his friends.

Henry Ward Beecher

Judge your neighbor by his best moments,
not his worst.

Bishop Fulton J. Sheen

Two things are bad for the heart —
running uphill and running down people.

Bernard Gimbel

They never raised a statue to a critic.

Martha Graham

Any fool can criticize, condemn, and complain, and most fools do.

Dale Carnegie

 $\mathbf{B}$ ecome genuinely interested
in other people.

Dale Carnegie

$\mathbf{H}$ ate is not the opposite of love; apathy is.

Rollo May

$\mathbf{B}$ e quick to praise.

Bernard Baruch

$\mathbf{A}$ man who lives for himself is a failure.

Norman Vincent Peale

$\mathbf{T}$ he man who lives by himself
and for himself is apt to be corrupted
by the company he keeps.

Charles Henry Parkhurst

The giving of love is
an education in itself.

Eleanor Roosevelt

Getting people to like you
is merely the other side of liking them.

Norman Vincent Peale

We awaken in others the same attitude
of mind we hold toward them.

Elbert Hubbard

Your opinion of others is apt to be
their opinion of you.

B. C. Forbes

Other people are like a mirror which
reflects back on us the kind of image we cast.

Bishop Fulton J. Sheen

Pity costs nothing and ain't worth nothing.
Josh Billings

The less you expect out of people,
the less you get.
Rudolph Giuliani

Count your blessings and
let your neighbor count his.
James Thurber

Pay less attention to what men say.
Just watch what they do.
Dale Carnegie

Nothing is more revealing than movement.
Martha Graham

Marriage is not just spiritual communion
and passionate embraces; marriage is also
three meals a day, sharing the work load and
remembering to take out the trash.

Dr. Joyce Brothers

When somebody's nice to you,
don't take advantage of it. You don't ride
a free horse to death.

Bessie & Sadie Delany

When you say something,
make sure you have said it. The chances
of your having said it are only fair.

E. B. White

There is only one terminal dignity — love.
And the story of a love is not important —
what is important is that one is capable
of love. It is perhaps the only glimpse
we are permitted of eternity.

Helen Hayes

Be honest with yourself
    so you will be honest with others.

Bernard Baruch

He who is able to love himself
    is able to love others also.

Paul Tillich

Friendship with oneself is all important,
  because without it one cannot be friends
    with anyone else in the world.

Eleanor Roosevelt

If you don't matter to you,
    it's hard to matter to others.

Malcolm Forbes

The most important single ingredient
    in the formula of success is knowing
      how to get along with people.

Theodore Roosevelt

You can close more business in two months
by becoming interested in other people
than you can in two years by trying
to get people interested in you.

Dale Carnegie

Do things for others and you'll find
your self-consciousness evaporating.

Dale Carnegie

Think as little as possible about yourself and
as much as possible about other people.

Eleanor Roosevelt

Nothing we do, however virtuous,
can be accomplished alone; therefore
we are saved by love.

Reinhold Niebuhr

Love becomes help.

Paul Tillich

Listening, not imitation, may be
      the sincerest form of flattery.
Dr. Joyce Brothers

The first duty of love is to listen.
Paul Tillich

When dealing with people, remember you
      are not dealing with creatures of logic,
      but with creatures of emotion.
Dale Carnegie

No man is whole of himself;
      his friends are the rest of him.
Harry Emerson Fosdick

If I don't have friends, then I ain't got nothin'.
Billie Holliday

The world is full of nice folks whatever color or religion. Your job is to find them.

Bessie & Sadie Delany

God grant me the serenity
to accept the things I
cannot change;
The courage to change
the things I can;
And the wisdom to know
the difference.

Rienhold Niebuhr

5

Hope

In the early days of television, a bishop named Fulton J. Sheen became a popular Tuesday night fixture on the DuMont Network. Sheen, like his fellow New York clergyman Norman Vincent Peale, believed in positive thinking.

Bishop Sheen once noted, "The mind is like a clock that is constantly running down. It has to be wound up daily with good thoughts."

If your mental timepiece is a little slow, turn the page for some stem-winding quotations. Armed with the wisdom that follows, you'll be able to take a licking and keep on ticking.

Hope is the mainspring of life.

Henry Stimson

The future belongs to those who believe
in the beauty of their dreams.

Eleanor Roosevelt

Ask the God who made you
to keep remaking you.

Norman Vincent Peale

Faith is the first requisite of success.

Elbert Hubbard

We need not fear the future for
the future will be in our own hands.

Thomas E. Dewey

Live from miracle
to miracle.

Artur Rubinstein

All growth is a leap in the dark.

Henry Miller

Plant the seeds of expectation
in your mind.

Norman Vincent Peale

They say you can't do it, but remember,
that doesn't always work.

Casey Stengel

Doubt isn't the opposite of faith;
it is an element of faith.

Paul Tillich

Fear freezes life.
Faith thaws it out.

Harry Emerson Fosdick

Humor is a prelude to faith,
and laughter is the beginning of prayer.

Reinhold Niebuhr

Freedom is the supreme good —
freedom from self-imposed limitation.

Elbert Hubbard

The greatest betrayals come from within.

Bishop Fulton J. Sheen

The greatest asset of a man, a business,
or a nation is faith.

Thomas J. Watson

6

Adversity

It is well known that New York can be a very tough place. Tough, but not impossible. Dorothy Parker observed, "As only New Yorkers know, if you can get through the twilight, you'll live through the night."

The following insights deal with the double-edged sword of adversity. New Yorkers understand the truth of Nietzsche's maxim, "That which does not kill me makes me stronger." To fully enjoy the glories of a lifetime in New York City, one must first endure and become strong.

Adversity

It is a mistake to think of failure
      as the enemy of success. Failure is
    a teacher — a harsh one, but the best.
                    Thomas J. Watson

A problem is an opportunity
         in work clothes.
                    Henry J. Kaiser

The art of living lies less in eliminating
   our troubles than in growing with them.
                    Bernard Baruch

God will not look you over
      for medals, degrees or diplomas,
          but for scars.
                    Elbert Hubbard

Show me a man who doesn't make mistakes,
and I'll show you a man
who doesn't do anything.

Theodore Roosevelt

In God's economy, nothing is wasted.
Through failure, we learn a lesson in humility
which is probably needed,
painful though it is.

Bill Wilson

Every problem has in it the seeds of its
own solution. If you don't have any problems,
you don't have any seeds.

Norman Vincent Peale

Difficulties should act as a tonic.
They should spur us to greater action.

B. C. Forbes

He who has never failed
cannot be great.
Failure is the truest
test of greatness.

Herman Melville

When we are worried, it is because
our subconscious mind is trying to telegraph
us some message of warning.

Bernard Baruch

If pleasures are greater in anticipation,
remember this is also true of trouble.

Elbert Hubbard

There are people who are always
anticipating trouble, and in this way,
they manage to enjoy many sorrows
that never really happen to them.

Josh Billings

The test of the heart is trouble.

Ella Wheeler Wilcox

When duty calls,
then is when character counts.

William Safire

Years ago, I used to commiserate
with people who suffered. Now I commiserate
only with those who suffer in ignorance,
who do not understand the purpose
and ultimate utility of pain.

Bill Wilson

You never know what you can do without
until you try.

Franklin Pierce Adams

Little minds are tamed and subdued
by misfortune, but great minds rise above it.

Washington Irving

Problems are the price you pay for progress.

Branch Rickey

'Tis easy enough to be pleasant,
     when life flows along like a song;
     But the man worthwhile
     is the one who will smile
     when everything goes dead wrong.

Ella Wheeler Wilcox

There is no failure except
     in no longer trying.

Elbert Hubbard

I know of no higher fortitude
     than stubbornness in the face
     of overwhelming odds.

Louis Nizer

The absence of alternatives
     clears the mind marvelously.

Henry Kissinger

7

Action

New Yorkers are not known for standing around; they are, above all, people of action. Perhaps no New York family has been more active in American life than the Roosevelts. Even their harshest critics must acknowledge the family's lasting impact on the American scene.

Franklin summed up the Roosevelt philosophy when he warned, "Above all, try something." Teddy, who was both uncle to Eleanor and sixth cousin to Franklin (but who's counting?) had a similar approach to life. His advice? "Do what you can with what you have, where you are."

The following words expound upon the proud New York tradition of getting things done. Now!

The first man gets the oyster. The second man gets the shell.

Andrew Carnegie

Discussion is a most excellent means
to avoid decision.
Bishop Fulton J. Sheen

Rhetoric is a poor substitute for action.
Theodore Roosevelt

The trouble is, if you don't risk anything,
you risk even more.
Erica Jong

Do and dare.

Dale Carnegie

Decision is a risk rooted in the courage
of being free.

Paul Tillich

Follow this simple rule:
If you can take the worst, take the risk.

Dr. Joyce Brothers

If I had my life to live over,
I'd make the same mistakes, only sooner.

Tallulah Bankhead

I am only one, but still I am one;
I cannot do everything, but I can do something;
and because I cannot do everything
I will not refuse to do the something
that I can do.

Edward Everett Hale

Happy people are those who
   have broken the chains of procrastination,
      those who find satisfaction
         in doing the job at hand.

Norman Vincent Peale

Concern should drive us into action and
         not into depression.

Karen Horney

If I feel depressed, I write my way out of it.

Bernard Malamud

If you rest, you rust.

Helen Hayes

Within us all are wells of thought and
dynamos of energy.

Thomas. J. Watson

Mix a conviction with a man and
something happens.

Adam Clayton Powell

There is nothing so useless as doing efficiently
that which should not be done at all.

Peter Drucker

Acting without thinking
is like shooting without aiming.

B. C. Forbes

8

Hard Work

In the late 1800s, Elbert Hubbard founded Roycroft Press in East Aurora. Hubbard authored a series of booklets that championed the principles of hard work and efficiency. He once advised, "Do your work with your whole heart, and you will succeed — there is so little competition."

Elbert Hubbard lost his life on the ill-fated *Lusitania* in 1915. That year, Bernard Baruch was earning a reputation as one of Wall Street's most savvy investors. Baruch's philosophy of personal finance was profoundly simple: "Work and save!"

If you're climbing the ladder of success, consider the advice of the following New Yorkers. They know each rung by heart.

Labor disgraces no man.
Unfortunately you occasionally find
some men who disgrace labor.

Ulysses S. Grant

Blessed is the man who has found his work.

Elbert Hubbard

No man needs sympathy because
he has to work. Far and away the best prize
that life offers is the chance to work hard
at work worth doing.

Theodore Roosevelt

It is better to be in love with your work
than in love with yourself.

B. C. Forbes

Luck is the residue of design.

Branch Rickey

If you have talent,
you will receive some measure of success —
but only if you persist.

Isaac Asimov

Think enthusiastically about everything,
especially your work.

Norman Vincent Peale

Get happiness out of your work,
or you may never know what happiness is.

Elbert Hubbard

Concentrate on your work,
and the applause will take care of itself.

B. C. Forbes

Industry is a better horse to ride
than genius.

Walter Lippmann

Be like a postage stamp — stick to one thing
until you get there.

Josh Billings

The world is an oyster, but you can't crack
it open on a mattress.

Arthur Miller

Nothing brings more satisfaction
than doing quality work.

Bessie Delany

The only sin is mediocrity.

Martha Graham

Hard Work

The price one pays
for pursing any profession or calling is
an intimate knowledge of its ugly side.

James Baldwin

The mode by which the inevitable
is reached is effort.

Felix Frankfurter

The harder you work,
the harder it is to surrender.

Vince Lombardi

Work:
1. That which keeps us out of trouble.
2. A plan of God to circumvent the devil.

Elbert Hubbard

The two kinds of people on earth are
the people who lift and the people who lean.

Ella Wheeler Wilcox

Laziness is like money —
the more of it you have, the more you want.
Josh Billings

Make the work interesting,
and discipline will take care of itself.
E. B. White

Let a human being throw the energies
of his soul into the making of something,
and the instinct of workmanship
will take care of his honesty.
Walter Lippmann

The world takes off its hat to those
who put in more than 50% of their capacity,
and stands on its head for those few and far
between souls who devote 100%.
Andrew Carnegie

Making a success of the job at hand is
the best step toward the kind of job you want.

Bernard Baruch

When troubles arise,
  wise men go to their work.

Elbert Hubbard

Anyone can do any amount of work,
  provided it isn't the work he is supposed
    to be doing at the moment.

Robert Benchley

There are no shortcuts to any place worth going.

Beverly Sills

When your work speaks for itself, don't interrupt.

Henry J. Kaiser

9

Success

Washington Irving once noted, "Great minds have purposes, others have wishes." In making this observation, Irving joined a long list of New Yorkers who have shared the secrets of successful living. On the following pages, we will examine the words of men and women who have achieved no small measure of success. Along with Irving, they remind us of this simple truth: There is more to living well than the wishing well.

Always aim for achievement,
and forget about success.

Helen Hayes

Real success consists in doing one's duty
well in the path where one's life is led.

Theodore Roosevelt

Of course there is no formula for success
except, perhaps, an unconditional acceptance
of life and what it brings.

Artur Rubinstein

Fame is a vapor, popularity an accident,
riches take wing. Only one thing endures,
and that is character.

Horace Greeley

Accomplishments have no color.

Leontyne Price

The secret of success is this:
>   There is no secret of success.
>>   *Elbert Hubbard*

There are no secrets to success.
>   It is the result of preparation, hard work,
>>   and learning from failure.
>>>   *Colin Powell*

Failure isn't making a mistake.
>   Failure is not cashing in on it.
>>   *Elbert Hubbard*

Success consists in the climb.
>   *Elbert Hubbard*

Excelsior!
>   *State Motto*

Success

Take the obvious, add a cupful of brains,
a generous pinch of imagination, a bucketful
of courage, and bring to a boil.

Bernard Baruch

When you want something, don't take
no for an answer. And when rejection comes,
don't take it personally.

Betty Furness

The way to succeed
is to double your failure rate.

Thomas J. Watson

How to succeed: Try hard enough.
How to fail: Try too hard.

Malcolm Forbes

Reason often makes mistakes,
> but conscience never does.

Josh Billings

Believe in yourself. Have faith in
your abilities. Without a humble but
reasonable confidence in your own powers,
you cannot be successful or happy.

Norman Vincent Peale

Whether it's dancing or living,
> learn by practice.

Martha Graham

Eighty percent of success is showing up.

Woody Allen

Enthusiasm makes ordinary people
extraordinary.

Norman Vincent Peale

Flaming enthusiasm, backed up
by horse sense and persistence, is the quality
that most frequently makes for success.

Dale Carnegie

The greatest accomplishments of man
have resulted from the transmission of ideas
and enthusiasm.

Thomas J. Watson

The real secret of success is enthusiasm.

Walter Chrysler

One machine can do the work
of fifty ordinary men. No machine can do
the work of one extraordinary man.

Elbert Hubbard

Time given to thought
is the greatest time saver of all.

Norman Cousins

Think.

Thomas J. Watson

Self-image sets the boundaries
of individual achievement.

Maxwell Maltz

A life that hasn't a definite plan
is likely to become driftwood.

David Sarnoff

When you plan and dream,
choose a suitable decision and hold to it.
Finish what you have begun.

E. B. White

You can't pick cherries
with your back
to the tree.

J. P. Morgan

10

Life

In 1888, Israel Baline was born in Temun, Russia. Like millions of others, young Israel accompanied his family to New York City. In time, he found a job as a singing waiter in the Bowery. Soon, Baline was writing songs and signing them with his new Americanized name, Irving Berlin.

Berlin, the man who wrote *God Bless America* and *White Christmas*, had a simple philosophy. He said, "Life is ten percent what you make it and ninety percent how you take it."

In this chapter, New Yorkers make sage observations on the human condition. Will these quotations be helpful? That depends upon you, because advice, like Berlin's view of life, is at least ninety percent how you take it.

Life is what we make it.
Always has been.
Always will be.

Grandma Moses

Man's main task in life
is giving birth to himself.

Erich Fromm

The best way to prepare for life
is to begin to live.

Elbert Hubbard

Live in the present.
That's where the fun is.

Donald Trump

Life is too good to waste a day.
It's up to you to make it sweet.

Sadie Delany

Destructiveness is the outcome
of unlived lives.

Erich Fromm

In the sea of life, it is the lightweights
who sink and the heavyweights who rise.

B. C. Forbes

One must never, for whatever reason,
turn his back on life.

Eleanor Roosevelt

The word "now" is like a bomb
through the window, and it ticks.

Arthur Miller

Life is a gamble,
but at least you play your own cards.

B. C. Forbes

It's a very short trip. While alive, live.
Malcolm Forbes

The art of living lies less in eliminating
our troubles than in growing with them.
Bernard Baruch

Life is what happens
while you are making other plans.
John Lennon

See each day as a chance
for something new to happen.
Sadie Delany

Age is not important unless
you're a cheese.
Helen Hayes

Life

I think somehow we learn who we really are
and live with that decision.

Eleanor Roosevelt

If you love life, life will love you back.

Artur Rubinstein

When you cease to make a contribution,
you begin to die.

Eleanor Roosevelt

Dying seems less sad
than having lived too little.

Gloria Steinem

Death is not the greatest loss in life.
The greatest loss is what dies inside
while we're alive.

Norman Cousins

There is only one you in all of time.
If you block your unique energy, it will never
exist through any other medium.

Martha Graham

The quality of a person's life is in direct
proportion to his commitment to excellence,
regardless of his chosen field of endeavor.

Vince Lombardi

When you come right down to it,
the secret of having it all is loving it all.

Dr. Joyce Brothers

Life is a tragedy,
full of joy.

Bernard Malamud

11

Wisdom

Thomas J. Watson was the driving force behind computer giant IBM. Watson observed, "Wisdom is the power that enables us to use knowledge for the benefit of ourselves and others." Walter Lippmann, the editor and essayist, wrote, "It requires wisdom to understand wisdom; the music is nothing if the audience is deaf."

The following quotations help us convert knowledge into wisdom so that we can appreciate more fully the subtle beauty of life's brief refrain.

Every man is a fool for at least five minutes
every day. Wisdom consists
in not exceeding that limit.

Elbert Hubbard

It's better to know nothing
than to know what isn't so.

Josh Billings

Nine-tenths of wisdom is being wise in time.

Theodore Roosevelt

Common sense is instinct,
and enough of it is genius.

Josh Billings

Wisdom consists in the anticipation
of consequences.

Norman Cousins

Experience is what enables you to recognize
a mistake when you make it again.

Earl Wilson

The only sense that is common
in the long run is the sense of change —
and we all instinctively avoid it.

E. B. White

Pick your books as you would your friends.
Have Emerson in your home. Ever see a movie
that was a bit over your head? Well, it was
because you haven't read enough.

Fiorello LaGuardia

It requires less mental energy to condemn
than to think.

Emma Goldman

Honesty, industry, concentration.

Andrew Carnegie

The trouble with most of us
is that we'd rather be ruined by praise
than saved by criticism.

Norman Vincent Peale

The best way to convince a fool that he is
wrong is to let him have his own way.

Josh Billings

It is better to know some of the questions
than to know all of the answers.

James Thurber

Intellectual sophistication can dry up
the wells of spiritual creativity.

Harry Emerson Fosdick

The man who does not do his own thinking
is a slave.

Robert Ingersoll

Patience is not only a virtue — it pays.

B. C. Forbes

No man is rich who wants more
than he has got.

Josh Billings

The greatest waste of money is to keep it.

Jackie Gleason

Constant effort and frequent mistakes are the stepping stones of genius.

Elbert Hubbard

12

Business Advice

New York City is the world's unquestioned business capital. Success in the business arena requires lots of insight, plenty of hard work and a dash of good fortune. But as E. B. White once observed, "No one should come to New York to live unless he is willing to be lucky."

The following quotations take us on an abbreviated tour through the world of business. Follow this advice, and you'll make enough of your own luck to live in New York as long as you like.

Money is a terrible master but an excellent servant.

P. T. Barnum

The less government interferes with private business, the better for general prosperity.

Martin Van Buren

A friendship founded on business is better than a business founded on friendship.

John D. Rockefeller

Never follow the crowd.

Bernard Baruch

The secret of success lies not in doing your own work, but in recognizing the right men to do it.

Andrew Carnegie

If you don't drive your business, you will be driven out of business.

B. C. Forbes

Whenever you see a successful business,
someone once made a courageous decision.

Peter Drucker

If you don't sell, it's not the product
that's wrong, it's you.

Estée Lauder

Don't borrow or lend;
but if you must do one, lend.

Josh Billings

I didn't choose my work.
My work chose me.

Richard Avedon

Marketing and innovation produce results;
all the rest are costs.

Peter Drucker

Advertising made me.

P. T. Barnum

Talent is only the starting point in business.
You've got to keep working that talent.

Irving Berlin

It takes 20 years to make
an overnight success.

Eddie Cantor

I never dreamed about success.
I worked for it.

Estée Lauder

I believe the true road to preeminent success
in any line is to make yourself
master of that line.

Andrew Carnegie

If you begin by denying yourself nothing,
the world is apt to do your denying for you.
Deny yourself or be denied.

B. C. Forbes

$\mathbf{A}$sk lots of questions and take lots of chances.
Only through curiosity can we discover
opportunities, and only by gambling
can we take advantage of them.

Clarence Birdseye

$\mathbf{D}$on't be afraid to give your best
to what seemingly are small jobs. If you
do the little jobs well, the big ones
will tend to take care of themselves.

Dale Carnegie

$\mathbf{I}$f you want to succeed, you should
strike out on new paths rather than travel
the old worn paths of accepted success.

John D. Rockefeller

$\mathbf{F}$ailure is success if we learn from it.

Malcolm Forbes

Find a need and fill it.

Ruth Stafford Peale

13

New York City

In all the world, there are only a handful of truly great cities, and New York qualifies. One mark of a great city is this: People can't seem to stop talking about it. Whether you're from upstate or out-of-state, whether you love New York or hate it, you certainly can't ignore it. In fact, so much has been written about New York City that little, it seems, remains unsaid.

For a sampling of good quotes about a great city, please turn the page.

The renowned and ancient city of Gotham.

Washington Irving

What is barely hinted at in other American cities is condensed and enlarged in New York.

Saul Bellow

New York: It is the icing on the pie called Christian Civilization.

H. L. Mencken

This great, plunging, dramatic, ferocious, swift, and terrible big city is the most folksy and provincial place I have lived in.

Alistair Cooke

The skyline of New York is a monument of splendor that no pyramids or palaces will ever equal or approach.

Ayn Rand

Everywhere outside New York City is Bridgeport, Connecticut.

Fred Allen

New York City

New Yorkers temperamentally
do not crave comfort and convenience.
If they did, they would live elsewhere.

E. B. White

If a man can live in Manhattan,
he can live anywhere.

Arthur C. Clarke

My first few weeks in New York were
an initiation into the kingdom of guts.

Shirley MacLaine

New Yorkers are funny, flippant, and feisty.
It's the only way to live there.

Audrey Meadows

When an American stays away from
New York too long, something happens to
him. Perhaps he becomes a little provincial,
a little dead, a little afraid.

Sherwood Anderson

Give my regards to Broadway.

George M. Cohan

There's *nothing* that can match Broadway.

Sammy Davis, Jr.

Broadway has been very good to me —
but then I've been very good to Broadway.

Ethel Merman

When you are away from Old Broadway,
you are only camping out.

George M. Cohan

New York City

Situated on an island, which I think it will
one day cover, it rises like Venice from the sea,
and, like the fairest of cities in the days of
her glory, receives into its lap tribute
of all riches of the earth.

Frances Trollope, 1832

What a place it is!
The number of ships beat me all hollow, and it
looked for all the world like a big clearing in
the West, with the dead trees still standing.

Davy Crockett

New York is perhaps the world's
great thoroughfare.

Walt Whitman

New York impressed me tremendously
because, more than any other city in the world,
it is the fullest expression of our modern age.

Leon Trotsky

There's no more crime in New York —
there's nothing left to steal.

Henny Youngman

I come from New York, where if you fall down,
someone will pick you up by your wallet.

Al McGuire

New York was something like
a circus performer walking a tightrope and
juggling at the same time. It could barely
maintain its position, but any movement
would tip the whole balance.

John V. Lindsay

It's not easy to impress a New Yorker.

Mike Royko

To me, New York was the pinnacle, the end-all
of the professional sporting world.

Mickey Mantle

New York City

Every true New Yorker believes
with all his heart that when a New Yorker
is tired of New York, he is tired of life.

Robert Moss

New York is not the cultural center
of America, but the business and
administrative center of American culture.

Saul Bellow

Other cities consume culture,
New York creates it.

Paul Goldberg

New York attracts the most talented people
in the world in the arts and professions.
It also attracts them in other fields.
Even the bums are talented.

Edmond Love

New York City isn't a melting pot,
it's a boiling pot.

Thomas E. Dewey

One of the truly great things
about being brought up in New York City
is that it allows you to go through life
with an open mind.

Jimmy Breslin

New York is a place of bounding,
exuberant diversity.

Edward Koch

Everybody ought to have
a Lower East Side in their lives.

Irving Berlin

You can take a boy out of Brooklyn,
but you can never get Brooklyn
out of the boy.

W. T. Ballard

Can we actually "know" the universe?
It's hard enough finding your way
around Chinatown.

Woody Allen

New York City

If you live in New York, even if you're Catholic,
you're Jewish.

Lenny Bruce

Many a New Yorker spends a lifetime
within the confines of an area smaller than a
country village. Let him walk two blocks from
his corner and he is in a strange land and
will feel uneasy until he gets back.

E. B. White

Living in New York City gives people
real incentives to want things
that nobody else wants.

Andy Warhol

To live in New York is a test
of valor and patience.

Audrey Meadows

I miss the animal buoyancy of New York,
the animal vitality.

Anaïs Nin

My favorite city in the world is New York.
Sure it's dirty — but like a beautiful lady
smoking a cigar.

Joan Rivers

New York is a diamond iceberg
floating in river water.

Truman Capote

No place has delicatessens like New York.

Judy Blume

Traffic signals in New York
are just rough guidelines.

David Letterman

It is a city where everyone mutinies,
but no one deserts.

Harry Hershfield

The world is grand,
awfully big and
astonishingly beautiful,
frequently thrilling.
But I love New York.

Dorothy Kilgallen

14

Politics

In New York, politics resembles mud wrestling: dirty work for the participants, but entertainment for everyone else. On the pages that follow, we'll hear from famous and infamous New York politicians. Some might even qualify as statesmen. As citizens in this great democracy, we prefer to be governed by statesmen. But it's much more fun to watch the politicians.

The way to have power is to take it.

"Boss" Tweed

In the truest sense, freedom cannot
be bestowed. It must be achieved.

Franklin D. Roosevelt

All the ills of democracy can be cured
by more democracy.

Alfred E. Smith

The United States is the greatest law factory
the world has ever known.

Charles Evans Hughes

You must not complicate your government
beyond the capacity of its electorate
to understand it.

Walter Lippmann

A technical objection
is the first refuge of a scoundrel.

Heywood Broun

The task is not to make the poor wealthy,
but productive.

Peter Drucker

There is no greater inequality
than the equal treatment of unequals.

Felix Frankfurter

Individual responsibility and personal freedom
are inevitably linked.

George Pataki

Thou shall not ration justice.

Learned Hand

The triumph of justice is the only peace.

Robert Ingersoll

Freedom can be retained by eternal vigilance
which has always been its price.

Elmer Davis

Justice is always in jeopardy.

Walt Whitman

Where else but in an American democracy
could a boy of the Lower East Side,
born in London to parents fleeing Russian
discrimination, grow up to be
a mayor of a pan-ethnic city?

Abraham Beame

This will remain the land of the free
only so long as it is the home of the brave.

Elmer Davis

When government accepts responsibility
for people, then people no longer take
responsibility for themselves.

George Pataki

In a neighborhood, as in life,
a clean bandage is much better
than a festering wound.

Edward Koch

We shall learn to be masters
of circumstances — or we shall be its victims.

Nelson A. Rockefeller

The greatest gift in political life, in any life,
is to view yourself objectively.

Hugh L. Carey

A reformer is a guy who rides
through a sewer in a glass-bottomed boat.

Jimmy Walker

Every public officer
should be recycled occasionally.

John V. Lindsay

<u>15</u>

Observations on Flowers, Music, a Clear Conscience And Other Joys of Life

We conclude with a wide range of thoughts on a wide range of topics. Enjoy.

I don't want to achieve immortality through my work. I want to achieve it through not dying.

Woody Allen

I would rather be the man
      who bought the Brooklyn Bridge
      than the one who sold it.

Will Rogers

Gossip is when you hear something
      you like about someone you don't.

Earl Wilson

Insanity is hereditary.
      You can get it from your children.

Sam Levenson

It is better to have loafed and lost
      than never to have loafed at all.

James Thurber

We are not tempted because we are evil.
We are tempted because we are human.

Bishop Fulton J. Sheen

We are not punished for our sins,
but by them.

Elbert Hubbard

Character is the result of two things —
mental attitude and the way
we spend our time.

Elbert Hubbard

It is much easier to repent of the sins
we have already committed than to repent
of those we intend to commit.

Josh Billings

A sleeping pill will never take the place
of a clear conscience.

Eddie Cantor

Anger blows out
the lamp of the mind.

Robert Ingersoll

No man can think clearly
when his fists are clenched.

George Jean Nathan

More people, on the whole,
are defeated by believing nothing
than by believing too much.

P. T. Barnum

A man is known by the company
his mind keeps.

Thomas Bailey Aldrich

The prime fallacy of pessimism is that
no one knows enough to be a pessimist.

Norman Cousins

Silence is the hardest argument to refute.

Josh Billings

The best argument seems
merely an explanation.

Dale Carnegie

A sharp tongue is the only edged tool
that grows keener with constant use.

Washington Irving

Misery is a communicable disease.

Martha Graham

Few men own their own property.
The property owns them.

Robert Ingersoll

Money is the root of every mess
you can think of.

Bessie Delany

Debt is a trap
which man sets and baits himself,
and then deliberately gets into.

Josh Billings

Flowers are heaven's masterpieces.

Dorothy Parker

All the sounds of the earth are like music.

Oscar Hammerstein, II

Every cubic inch of space is a miracle.

Walt Whitman

The first hour of the morning
is the rudder of the day.

Henry Ward Beecher

Four things I am wiser to know:
idleness, sorrow, a friend, and a foe.
Dorothy Parker

Middle age is when you've met
so many people that every new person
you meet reminds you of someone else.
Ogden Nash

The hardest years in life are those
between ten and seventy.
Helen Hayes

Diets are for those who are thick
and tired of it.
Mary Tyler Moore

One ship drives east and another west,
with the self same winds that blow;
'tis the set of the sails and not the gales
that determines where they go.

Ella Wheeler Wilcox

Enthusiasm is the all-essential
human jet propellant.

B. C. Forbes

Some men succeed by what they know;
some by what they do; and
a few by what they are.

Elbert Hubbard

One worthwhile task, carried to
a successful conclusion, is worth
a half-a-hundred half-finished tasks.

Malcolm Forbes

Every opportunity is an obligation;
      every possession a duty.
                      John D. Rockefeller, Jr.

Any man who is a bear on the future
      of this country will go broke.
                      J. P. Morgan

Self-image sets the boundaries
      of individual accomplishment.
                      Maxwell Maltz

Men can starve
      from a lack of self-realization as much
      as they can from lack of bread.
                      Richard Wright

All men should strive to learn
before they die what they are running from,
and to, and why.

James Thurber

It is better to light a candle
than to cause the darkness.

Eleanor Roosevelt

It's a great advantage to be a late bloomer.
All the pressures are off.

Beverly Sills

Strong people always have
strong weaknesses.

Peter Drucker

Flattery is like cologne, to be smelt of,
        not swallowed.

Josh Billings

Nobody will ever win the battle of the sexes.
        There's too much fraternizing
            with the enemy.

Henry Kissinger

An expert is one who knows more and more
        about less and less.

Nicholas Murray

When a subject becomes totally obsolete,
        we make it a required course.

Peter Drucker

There's something satisfying about cleaning
        as long as you're not in a rush.

Sadie Delany

Be sincere, be brief, be seated.

Franklin D. Roosevelt

Sources

About the Author

Criswell Freeman is a Doctor of Clinical Psychology living in Nashville, Tennessee. He is the author of *When Life Throws You a Curveball, Hit It* and *The Wisdom Series* from WALNUT GROVE PRESS. He is also a published country music songwriter.